Learn

a little

Spanish

with

sangría

Lisa in the process of preparing Sangría.

¡Looks like we're in for a fun night!

🍷

Learn a little Spanish with Sangría

By Serge Seveau

Publisher; Serge Seveau

Published 2011 in electronic format

Published 2015 in print format

First Print: 2015

Print ISBN: 978-0-9871623-6-6

Website: seveau.net

This book drew inspiration from my desire to have fun learning Spanish; and enjoy the diverse range of Sangría Lisa and I consume on our trips to Spain visiting family.

salud

Let's get stuck into it - We are here to enjoy Sangría *(love that stuff)*, and of course, learn a little Spanish along the way - ¡how good is that! The best thing is that Sangría encourages people to practice their 'newly learnt language' - ¡win win! - (or: wine wine) . . . Having said that, keep in mind alcoholic beverages must at all times be consumed/served in a responsible manner.

Kill the '*cheap*' myth - It would seem that most people think of Sangría as a 'red wine punch' made with the cheapest wine at hand. This holds true if waking up with a shocking hangover is your idea of enjoying a drink with your meal! The truth is simple; if you wouldn't drink a wine on its own - because it's crap - then don't use it to 'create' a beverage that is meant to complement and enhance the taste of the beautiful food prepared. So, make sure you use a decent *vino tinto* (Red wine).

The great thing about learning Spanish is that letters of the alphabet are always pronounced the same - *phonemic orthography*. For example, in English the letter 'i' is pronounced differently in 'win' and 'wine'. If you know how to pronounce the alphabet in Spanish you can easily sound out all words, making Spanish very easy to read (there is an alphabet - pronunciation section towards the end).

¡They're here! - Your guests arrive and you greet them with "Hola" (OH-lah); it is spelled 'hola' (hello) but the 'h' is always silent in Spanish. Also, you may or may not know, but in Spain there is a formal and informal way of speaking. We are going to use the informal version, two reasons;

1. You are likely to be talking to friends only, and

2. From personal experience, when in Spain, every time I use the formal Spanish I am told not to bother...go figure...

So, you have warmly welcomed your guests. They are here to taste your creation, brew, concoction, your work-of-art, your *Sangría*. Excitedly they return the same "hola". You want to know how they are, so you ask:

You: "¿Cómo estás?" (¿koh-moh ehs-tahs?) (how are you?) - to that your guest replies:

Guest: "Muy bien, gracias." (mwee byehn, grah-syahs) (Very well, thank you)

Okay - ¡I hear ya! - The ¿ and the ? simply means the question starts ¿ and finishes ? - a little bit like "quotation marks" indicate the beginning and end of a quotation - easy - the same goes for ¡ and ! - it just simply indicates the beginning and end of a sudden remark.

¿*Tapas* - or not - *Tapas*? - The famous Spanish Tapas is not Tapas until something very special happens; Lisa and I, during our travels through Spain, have been served; (amongst an endless number of beverages); patatas fritas, mixed nuts, prawn chips, chicken paella, olives, pig snout, salami and tomato on bread, tuna and tomato roll, vol-au-vents, tiny toasts with seafood spread, pork crackle chips, tomato paste and onion pasties and at last but not least - ¡Nada! (nothing).

But, the one and all important aspect of Tapas - the one and only truly differentiating and identifiable feature that separates a Tapas from an ordinary and boring dish just sitting on the cooking bench awaiting it's consumption by the devourer anxiously wanting to achieve absolute pallet satisfaction, the disguisable characteristic that isolates Tapas from appetizer, starter, finger food, first course, nibbles, 'hors d'oeuvres' -- ¡*the vesicle*! -- yes; once the food has been placed in a small brown dish it miraculously transforms into Tapas. This vesicle can be

4

made from glass, clay, cane, that doesn't seem to be of any importance. But, it must be small and brown - go figure . . . So, to keep things genuine, find a brown, earth/clay dish and, 'Voilà' - your Tapas looks authentic - and now, a perfect complement for your Sangría.

¡You know more Spanish than you think! - What if I told you, you already know hundreds of Spanish words? What if English words were the same in Spanish (just pronounced differently)?

Well, there are many words that are the same. Let's take "celebration" - in Spanish it is "celebración" - all we did is change the **-tion** with **-ción** - how easy is that. There are hundreds like this, and they are known as cognates: words of a common origin.

For example:

situation – situación (see-to-ah-siohn)
separation – separación (seh-pah-rah-siohn)
celebration – celebración (seh-leh-bra-siohn)
conversation – conversación (con-behr-sah-siohn)
consideration – consideración (con-si-deh-rah-siohn)
transformation – transformación (trans-fohrm-ah-siohn)

What if the English word ends in **-or**
Well, it's even easier: for example,
actor – actor (ahk-tohr)
color – color (koh-lohr)
doctor – doctor (dock-tohr)
director – director (dee-reck-tohr)

and, if the English word ends in **-al**, then, believe it or not:
-al stays as **-al**
local – local (loh-cahl)
usual – usual (u-ju-ahl)
moral – moral (moh-rahl)
animal – animal (ah-nee-mahl)
natural – natural (nah-to-rahl)

general – general (kheh-neh-rahl)
hospital – hospital (ohs-pee-tahl)
criminal – criminal (cree-mee-nahl)

¡How good is that!

-ism becomes **-ismo**:
organism – organismo (or-gah-nee-smoh)
optimism – optimismo (ohp-tee-meez-moh)
mechanism – mecanismo (meh-kah-neez-moh)

-nce becomes **-ncia**
patience – paciencia (pah-si-en- thya)
arrogance – arrogancia (ah-ro-gan- thya)
experience - experiencia (eks-peh-ree-**an**-thya)
ambulance - ambulancia (am-boo-**lan**-thya)

¡See! You know a lot more Spanish than you thought. Just a few more - just to get really excited . . . *¿is it time to drink that Sangría yet?*   ;-)

-ty becomes **-dad**
identity - identidad (ee-den-tee-**dad**)
curiosity - curiosidad (koo-rio-si-**dad**)
electricity - electricidad (eh-lek-tree-thee-**dad**)

-ive becomes **-ivo**
active - activo (ak-**tee**-boh)
decisive - decisivo (deh-thee-**see**-boh)
effective - efectivo (eh-fehk-**tee**-boh)

-ous becomes **-oso**
gracious - gracioso (grah-cee-**oh**-soh)
delicious - delicioso (deh-lee-cee-**oh**-soh)
ambitious - ambicioso (am bee cee-**oh** soh)

and yes, **-ble** stays as **-ble**
terrible - terrible (teh-**ree**-bleh)
admirable - admirable (ahd-mee-**ra**-bleh)
impossible - imposible (im-poh-**thee**-bleh)

You know so much Spanish, ¡this is great!

You: "Would you like some Sangría?" *"¿Quieres un poco la Sangría?" (KYEH-res oon pohcoh lah Sangría)*

Guest: "Yes, a glass, please." *"Si, un vaso, por favor" (see, oon bah-soh, por fa-bohr)*

Guest: "Thank you very much." *"Muchas gracias" (moo-chas gra-thyas)*

You: "Don't mention it." *"De nada." (deh na-da)*

Guest: "I love Sangría." *"Me encanta la Sangría" (mi en-can-ta la San-gria)*

You: "Me too." *"también" (tahm-bee-ehn)*

9

Your guest has brought an unexpected friend, and you want to know his name. You ask:

You: "¿Cómo te llamas?" (coh-moh teh ya-mas?) (literally means: how are you called?).

Friend: "Me llamo Mark." (meh ya-moh Mark)

You: "Nice to meet you Mark." "Mucho gusto Mark." (moo-choh goo-stoh Mark)

Friend: "Enchanted." "Encantado." (en-kan-tah-doh)

¡Look at you go! What's needed are those yellow sticky notes plastered all over the house; each with the name of what it is stuck on. Each time you look at it you have to say it out loud - that really works well. On the frigo (fridge) put lots of 'stickies' with both the English and Spanish words for the contents of the frigo; and all cupboards as well. To help you with this, there is a mini dictionary at the end of the book.

¡Surely it's time to drink Sangría! Soon, but first, keep in mind there are sections towards the back of the book where you can learn such things as Numbers, Months, Week days, Colors, Foods, etc.

And of course, what about some simple everyday words:

•Mr	Señor (se-nyor)
•Mrs	Señora (se-nyo-ra)
•Miss	Señorita (se-nyo-ri-ta)
•yes	si (see
•no	no (noh)
•good morning	buenos diás (bwe-nohs dee-ahs)
•good evening	buenas tardes (bwe-nas tar-des)
•of course	claro (cla-ro)
•okay!	¡vale! (ba-leh)
•maybe	quizás (kee-thahs)
•come here	vien aquí (bee-n ah-kee)
•look	mira (mee-ra)
•where	Donde (don-deh)

•cheers!   ¡Salud! (sah-lood)

•something else?   ¿algo más? (ahl-goh
mahs)

•nothing else   nada más (nah-dah
mahs)

•the pleasure is mine. el gusto es mio (el
goo-stoh s mee-oh)

13

'Hasta la vista' is a no no . . . people just
don't say it in Spain. What is used in Spain
is:

- see you later   hasta luego (as-ta loo-
e-go)
- see you soon   hasta pronto (as-sta
pron-toh)
- see you tomorrow   hasta mañana (as-ta
ma-nya-na)
- goodbye   adiós (a-dyos)

~ ? ~ ¡ Sangría time ¡ ~ ? ~

'Just one last thing' - Most words have a
gender, that is, they are male or female.
Either they end in **'o'** (sometimes **'e'**) for male
or they end in **'a'** for female.

For example:
a dog	un perr**o**
the dog	el perr**o**
a cat	un gat**o**
the cat	el gat**o**

14

enchanted	for a male - encantad**o**
enchanted	for a female - encantad**a**
an apple	una manzan**a**
the apple	la manzan**a**
a bottle	una botell**a**
the bottle	la botell**a**

The second *'just one last thing'* - when we speak English we start by saying 'who', then what is happening, such as: "I eat", "You eat", "He eats". When we speak Spanish it's the other way around, we change how the word ends;

To eat	com**er**
I eat	com**o**
He eats	com**e**
You eat	com**es**
They eat	com**en**

To live	viv**ir**
I live	viv**o**
He lives	viv**e**

| You live | viv**es** |
| They live | viv**en** |

¡The wooden spoon thing! To ensure an authentic look to your Sangría, always use the same wooden spoon. Whenever you create a Red wine Sangría, stir your creation with the same wooden spoon at all times, never really washed but simply rinsed; in time the spoon takes on a deep red appearance - just like the ones seen in 'Spanish Bars'.

¡The *Lemonade or Tonic Water* thing!

Personally, I much prefer the taste of Lemonade over Tonic water – that added sweetness; and as such never use Tonic water, just Lemonade - and for best and most refreshing results, I add the Lemonade just prior to drinking the Sangría; that way you don't lose any of the bubbles (guaranteed to taste much better).

¡The Ice Cube thing! I find large ice cubes do a much better job than smaller ones. They have a smaller surface area and as such your Sangría doesn't get 'watered down' as fast (if you paint a brick and then break the brick in half, you now have two more surfaces to paint - therefore, the smaller the object, the larger the surface area - relatively speaking).

In the Sangría recipes grams are used, as a rule of thumb, if 100 grams of sugar is used, that is just under ½ cup (more or less and close enough).

RED SANGRÍA RECIPES

This recipe is my favorite and the simplest. It has no name because Lisa (my wife) came up with it - after extensive experimenting, tasting and consuming delicious Sangría . . . Let's call it:

Lisa's (love) Potion

1 bottle Red Wine
125 ml Cointreau
125 gm of Sugar
125 ml lemon Juice
600 ml of Lemonade
Lemon slices (10 or so) cut in half
Large ice cubes

Pour the bottle of Wine in a carafe.

Add all ingredients (not Lemonade or Ice) and stir until all the Sugar is dissolved (or let sit overnight). Keep it in the fridge until ready for consumption.

Add Lemonade and ice just before drinking - ¡listo! (ready)

Sangría Flamenca

1 bottle Red Wine
250 ml Pedro Ximènez
1 Orange
1 Lemon
1 Peach
50 gm of Sugar
Large Ice Cubes

Pour in a large pitcher a bottle or Wine.

Add Sugar and bits of Orange and lemon - Press with your hands so that they release all their juices, also add the chopped peaches.

Finally, add the ice, very abundant and in large chunks, and add the Pedro Ximènez. ¡Listo! Ready to serve.

Liquor Sangría

1 bottle Red Wine
250 ml of Lemonade
250 ml Orange Soda
125 ml of Peach Liquor
125 ml of Apple Liquor
250 ml Cointreau
250 ml of Red Vermouth
2 Apples,   2 Peaches
1 Pear,   1 Lemon
Large Ice Cubes

Put the Wine, Orange soda and Lemonade in a pitcher.

Add the Sugar and all the liquors.

After putting in all the ingredients, give them a good stir; add all the fruits chopped into cubes.

Leave in the fridge for a few hours and add ice cubes before serving - ¡Salud!

Asturian Sangría

1 bottle Red Wine
125 ml of Brandy
200 ml of Orange Juice
125 ml of Lemon Juice
3 Apples
2 Oranges
½ a Lemon
1 Lemon Peel in spiral
50 gm of Sugar
1 Cinnamon Stick
Large Ice Cubes

Peel and chop fruit into small pieces.

Put all the fruit in a pitcher and add Sugar and Brandy. Then add the Cider, Orange Juice and Lemon Juice.

Add the Cinnamon Stick and Lemon Peel Spiral. Put it in the fridge several hours to absorb the flavor of the fruit. Add Ice Cubes before serving.

Red Summer Wine Sangría

½ bottle of Red Wine
500 ml of Soda (or Lemonade)
Lemon Slices
Vermouth Rosso
Large Ice Cubes

Enter the ice in a pitcher and then introduce the Wine.

The put the soda and spray with a splash of Red Vermouth (amount to taste).

Enter the lemon slices and is ready to serve - ¡Salud!

Bomb Sangría

1 bottle Red Wine
250 ml Orange Soda
250 ml Lemonade
125 ml Gin
125 ml Vermouth
125 ml Whiskey
60 ml Tequila
2 Apples
2 Peaches
1 Banana
1 Pear
1 Lemon
100 gm of Sugar
Large Ice Cubes

Chop the fruit, removing the skin before, and once cut, put together with the Wine in a bowl with capacity for more than 2 liters.

Add the Sugar and then pour in the Wine and soft drinks.

Stir everything and add the Gin, Vermouth, Whiskey and Tequila.

Then put it in the fridge and let cool a few hours.

Add ice cubes before serving - Enjoy!

Melon Sangría

1 bottle Red Wine
200 ml Whiskey
500 ml Lemonade
50 gm Sugar
2 slices of Melon (white flesh)
Large Ice Cubes

Peel the Melon slices and cut it into cubes.

Pour into a 2 liter jug. Add the Sugar and then add the Whiskey.

Add Wine and Lemonade. Mix everything. Cool in the fridge for a few hours and add ice cubes before serving - Enjoy!

Typical Sangría

1 bottle Red Wine
200 ml Orange Juice
200 ml Lemon Juice
100 ml Cointreau
2 Peaches
1 Orange
1 Apple
80 gm Sugar
Lemon Pulp
Large Ice Cubes

Pour the Wine into a jug with the Sugar and mix.

Pour the Orange juice and Lemon juice.

Cut the Peaches, Orange and Apple into pieces and put them into the jar. Add a splash of Cointreau to your taste.

Leave in the fridge cooling and absorbing the flavor of the fruit. A few hours later, add ice cubes into the jug and serve. - Enjoy!

Cognac Sangría

1 bottle Red Wine
125 ml Cognac
250 ml Soda (or Lemonade)
50 gm Sugar
1 Pear
2 Apples
1 Lemon
100 gm Cherries
½ Cinnamon Stick
½ Orange Zest
½ Lemon Zest
Large Ice Cubes

Peel all fruits, cut the Apples and Lemons into slices and Pears into quarters, add the cherries, and put it all in a jar.

Cover the fruit with the Wine, add Cinnamon Stick, Orange and Lemon Zest and leave for about 1 hour.

30

After this time, add the Sugar, the Brandy and the Soda.

Let stand for a while longer.   Before serving add Ice Cubes - Ready!

Brandy Sangría

1 bottle Red Wine
125 ml Lemon Juice
4 Peaches
2 Oranges
1 Cinnamon Stick
125 ml Brandy
50 gm Sugar
Large Ice Cubes

Chop Peaches and Oranges and put them in a bowl with the Sugar and Brandy.

Gently mix, then add the Wine, Lemon Juice and the Cinnamon Stick.

Put in the fridge and allow chilling. When serving add Ice - ¡listo!

Sangría of White Wine

1 bottle White Wine
500 ml of Soda (or Lemonade)
125 ml of Cointreau
2 Peaches
1 Apple
1 Pear
1 Orange
½ a Pineapple
1 Lemon
50 gm Sugar
Large ice cubes

Put the Wine into a large pitcher, squeeze the lemons and mix it with the Wine.

Chop all fruit into small cubes and add to the preparation.

Add the Sugar, Cointreau and Nutmeg.

Let stand several hours in a cold place.

When serving add ice cubes and soda. Mix and serve.

Cava Sangría

1 bottle of Cava Brut
125 ml Brandy
125 ml Cointreau
250 ml Lemonade
250 ml Orange Soda
50 gm Sugar
100 gm Strawberries
1 Peach
1 Orange
Large Ice Cubes

Chop the fruit.

Put the Soda and Liqueur in a pitcher.

Add the cava and then the Sugar.

Allow few hours in the fridge and when serving put some ice cubes.

Mixed Sangría

½ a bottle White Wine
½ a bottle Red Wine
1 stick of Cinnamon
2 Peaches
2 Apples
1 Lemon
100 gm of Strawberry
50 gm of Sugar
Large Ice Cubes

Chop the fruit and put it together with the two kinds of Wine in a jug.

Add the cinnamon stick and Sugar.

Leave in fridge to marinate for a few hours.

Add ice cubes before serving.

Days:

today	hoy (oy)
yesterday	ayer (ah-YEHR)
tomorrow	mañana (mah-NYAH-nah)
week	semana (seh-MAH-nah)
month	mesa (meh-sah)

All days of the week are in lower case letter:

Monday	lunes (LOO-nehs)
Tuesday	martes (MAHR-tehs)
Wednesday	miércoles (MYEHR-koh-lehs)
Thursday	jueves (WEH-vehs)
Friday	viernes (VYEHR-nehs)
Saturday	sábado (SAH-bah-doh)
Sunday	domingo (doh-MEEN-goh)

Alphabet pronunciation:

a	sounds like - how **are** you
b	b and v both sound like **b**
c	**ca** sounds like **Kah**
c	**co** sounds like **Koh**
c	**cu** sounds like **Koo**
c	sounds like **th** if before **i**
c	sounds like **th** if before **e**
ch	sounds like **ch**eese
d	**d**esk
e	**e**splanade
f	**f**actory

g	**ge**	sounds like **Hreh**
g	**gi**	sounds like **Hree**
g	**gen**	sounds like **hren**
g	**ga**	sounds like normal **g**
g	**go**	sounds like normal **g**
g	**gu**	sounds like normal **g**

h	silent, as in honor
i	**i** = pol**i**ce
i	**ia** = **ya**

i	**ie** = **yeh**
i	**io** = **yoh**
j	**h**ome
k	**k**ilo
l	**l**eg
ll	**y**ou
m	**m**other
n	**n**ever
ñ	ca**ny**on
o	**o**h
p	**p**en
q	**c**an
r	b**r**ick
rr	to**rr**o zo**rr**o
s	**s**oup
t	**t**ent
u	t**oo**l
v	**b**ed
w	**w**ord
x	**h**iss
y	s**ee**
z	**th**ink

Numbers:

0	cero	(SEH-roh)
1	uno	(OO-noh)
2	dos	(dohs)
3	tres	(trehs)
4	cuatro	(KWAH-troh)
5	cinco	(SEEN-koh)
6	seis	(SEH_ees)
7	siete	(see_EH-teh)
8	ocho	(OH-choh)
9	nueve	(noo_EH-beh)
10	diez	(dee_EHS)
11	once	(OHN-seh)
12	doce	(DOH-seh)
13	trece	(TREH-seh)
14	catorce	(kah-TOHR-seh)
15	quince	(KEEN-seh)
16	dieciséis	(dee_EH-see SEH-ees)
17	diecisiete	(dee EHsee seeEH-teh)
18	dieciocho	(dee EH-see_OH-choh)
19	diecinueve	(dee E-seeNOOEH-beh)
20	veinte	(BAIN-teh)
21	veintiuno	(BAIN-tee-OO-noh)
22	veintidós	(BAIN-tee-DOHS)
23	veintitrés	(BAIN-tee-TREHS)

30	treinta	(TRAIN-tah)
40	cuarenta	(kwah-REHN-tah)
50	cincuenta	(seen-KWEHN-tah)
60	sesenta	(seh-SEHN-tah)
70	setenta	(seh-TEHN-tah)
80	ochenta	(oh-CHEHN-tah)
90	noventa	(noh-BEHN-tah)
100	cien	(see-EHN)
200	doscientos	(dohs-see-EHN-tohs)
300	trescientos	(trehs-see-EHN-tohs)
500	quinientos	(kee-nee-EHN-tohs)
1000	mil	(MEEL)

Months:

All the months in Spanish are written in lower case letters.

January	enero (eh-NEH-roh)
february	febrero (feh-BREH-roh)
march	marzo (MAR-soh)
april	abril (ah-BREEL)
may	mayo (MAH-joh)
june	junio (HOO-nyoh)
july	julio (HOO-lyoh)
august	agosto (ah-GOHS-toh)
september	septiembre (sehp-TYEHM-breh)
october	octubre (ohk-TOO-breh)
november	noviembre (noh-VYEHM-breh)
december	diciembre (dee-SYEHM-breh)

Family:

Family	familia (fah-mee-lia)
father	padre (pah-dreh)
mother	madre (mah-dreh)
grandfather	abuelo (ah-boo-eh-lo)
grandmother	abuela (ah-boo-eh-lah)
brother	hermano (air-mah-noh)
sister	hermana (air-mah-nah)
uncle	tío (ti-oh)
aunt	tía (ti-ah)

Colors:

black	negro (NEH-groh)
white	blanco (BLAHN-koh)
gray	gris (GREES)
red	rojo (ROH-hoh)
blue	azul (ah-THOOL)
yellow	amarillo (ah-mah-REE-yoh)
green	verde (BEHR-deh)
Orange	naranja (nah-RAHN-hah)
purple	púrpura (POOR-poo-rah)
pink	rosa (ROH-sah)
brown	marrón (mahr-ROHN)

Eating:

plate	plato (PLAH-toh)
spoon	cuchara (koo-CHAH-rah)
fork	tenedor (teh-NEH-dohr)
knife	cuchillo (koo-CHEE-yoh)
drinking glass	vaso (BAH-soh)
cup/mug	taza (TAH-sah)
saucer	platillo (plah-TEE-yoh)
napkin	servilleta (sehr-bee-YEH-tah)
à la carte	a la carta (ah lah KAHR-tah)
breakfast	desayuno (deh-sah-YOO-noh)
lunch	comida (koh-MEE-dah)
dinner	cena (SEH-nah)

Food:

chicken	pollo (POH-yoh)
beef	ternera (tehr-NEH-rah)
fish	pescado (pehs-KAH-doh)
ham	jamón (hah-MOHN)
sausage	salchicha (sahl-CHEE-chah)

cheese	queso (KEH-soh)
eggs	huevos (oo-WEH-bohs)
salad	ensalada (ehn-sah-LAH-dah)
vegetables	verdura (behr-DOO-rah)
fruit	fruta (FROO-tah)
bread	pan (pahn)
toast	tostada (tohs-TAH-dah)
rice	arroz (AHR-rohs)
beans	frijoles (free-HOH-lehs)
coffee	café (kah-FEH)
tea	té (TEH)
juice	zumo (THOO-mo)
water	agua (ah-GWAH)
beer	cerveza (sehr-BEH-sah)
red wine	vino tinto (BEE-noh TEEN-toh)
white wine	vino blanco (BEE-noh-BLAHNkoh)
salt	sal (sahl)
pepper	pimienta (pee-MYEHN-tah)
butter	mantequilla (mahn-teh-KEE-yah)
bottle	botella (boh-TEH-yah)
whiskey	whisky (WEES-kee)
vodka	vodka (BOHD-kah)
rum	ron (rohn)
tonic water	agua tónica (AHgwahTOHneekah)
coca-cola	coca-cola (KOH-kah-KOH-lah)
orange juice	zuma de naranja (THOOmah deh NAHrahnhah)

Mini Word Translator:

A a

acorn	bellota
add	añadir
almonds	almendras
anchovy	anchoa
Apple	manzana
arrange	poner
artichoke	alcachofa
asparagus	espárrago
aspic	aspic, galantina
aubergine	berenjena
avocado	aguacate palta

B b

bacon	beicón
bake	cocer al horno
baking powder	levadura (en polvo)
banana	plátano
barbeque	barbacoa
basil	albahaca
bass (sea bass)	lubina
basting	rociando

batter	albardilla
bayleaf	laurel
beans	habas
beef	ternera
beetroot	remolach
bitter	agrio/ácido
black beans	alubias negras
blackberry	mora
blade of a knife	hoja del cuchillo
blanch	escaldar
blancmange	crema de maizena
boil	hervir
boiling point	punto de ebullición
bone	hueso/espina
boned	dehuesado
borage	borraja
bowl	cuenco
brandy	coñac
bread	pan
breadboard	tabla de cortar el pan
breadcrumbs	migas de pan
bread stick	grisín
breakfast	desayuno
breast (of chicken)	pechuga
broad beans	habas
broccoli	brócoli
broth	caldo
brown	dorar

brown bread	pan integral
brush	v. cepillar n.cepillo
brussel sprouts	coles de Bruselas
butter	mantequilla

C c

cabbage	col
cake	pastel
can	lata
canneloni	canelones
capers	alcaparras
carrot	zanahoria
carve (meat)	trinchar la carne
casserole	estofado
cauliflower	coliflor
cayenne pepper	pimienta cayena
celery	apio
cheese	queso
cheesecake	tarta de queso
chestnut	castaño
chicken	pollo
chick peas	garbanzos
chill	enfriar
chips	patata frita
chive (herb)	chive (hierba)

chocolate	chocolate
chop (cut up)	picar
chop	chuleta, costilla
cider	sidra
cinnamon	canela
clams	almejas
clove	clavo (de olor)
cloves of garlic	dientes de ajo
coat	rebozar
coarse	de grano grueso
cocoa powder	cocoa (en polvo)
coconut	coco
coconut milk	leche de coco
cod	bacalao
combine	combinar
conger eel	congrio
consistency	consistencia
cook	cocinar
cooked ham	jamón York
cookie	galleta
coriander	cilantro
cottage cheese	requesón
cornflour	harina de maíz
courgette	calabacín
cover	cubrir
crab	cangrejo
cranberry	arándano
crayfish	langosta

cream	nata
cream (single cream)	nata líquida
cream (double cream)	nata para montar
cream (whipped cream)	nata montada
crisps	patatas fritas
crispy	crocante
crouton	cuscurro
cucumber	pepino
curdle	cuajar
cumin	comino

D d

dash	chorrito
dent	hueco
dessert	postre
diced	cortar en cuadritos
diet	dieta
dill	eneldo
dining room	comedor
dining-room table	mesa de comedor
dinnertime	hora de cenar
dip	sumergir
dish	plato
dough	masa
doughnut	donut

drain	escurrir
dress (salad)	aliñar
dressing	aliño
drumstick	muslo de pollo
dry	secar
duck	pato

E e

edge	borde
egg	huevo
eggcup	huevera
eggplant	berenjena
egg white	clara de huevo
egg yolk	yema de huevo
empty	vaciar
enchilada	enchilada
endives	endibias

F f

fennel	hinojo
fillets	filetes
filling	relleno
finely	en trozos menudos

fish	pescado
flatten	aplanar
flesh	carne
flour	harina
foam	espuma
food	comida
food coloring	colorante alimenticio
fold	doblar
fork	tenedor
freeze	congelar
freezer	congelador
french fries	patatas fritas
fridge	frigo
frozen	congelado
fruit	fruta
fry	freír
frying pan	sartén

G g

garlic	ajo
garnish	guarnición
gelatin	gelatina
get rid of	quitar
gherkins	pepinillo
ginger	jengibre

glaze	glasear
golden	dorado
goose	ganso
gooseberry	grosella espinosa
gourmet	gourmet, gastrónomo
gradually	lentamente
granulated sugar	azúcar granulada
grape	uva
grapefruit	pomelo
grated	rallado
grease	grasa
greased	engrasado
grease (with butter)	enmantequillar
grease (with oil)	aceitar
greaseproof paper	papel encerado
greengage	ciruela claudia
greengrocer	verdulero
green pepper	pimiento verde
green beans	habichuelas
griddle	plancha
gridiron	parrilla
ground	molido
grill	gratinar
grind	machacar
gristle	cartílago
gruel	gachas
guava	guayaba

H h

haddock	abadejo
hake	merluza
halve	dividir en dos
ham	jamón
handful	puñado
hard-boiled egg	huevo duro
hare	liebre
heart	corazon
heat	calentar
herb	hierba
herb garden	herbario
herring	arenque
honey	miel

I i

ice cream	helado
icing Sugar	azúcar glace
ingredients	ingredientes
instead of	en vez de

J j

jam	mermelada
jam jar	tarro para mermelada
jelly (as dessert)	gelatina
juice	zumo
juicy	jugoso
junket	leche cuajada
junk food	comida basura

K k

kidney beans	alubias rojas
kidney	riñon
kipper	arenque
kitchen	cocina
kitchen foil	papel de aluminio
kitchen sink	fregadero
kitchenware	artículos de cocina
kitchen tissue	papel de cocina
kiwi	un kiwi
knife	cuchillo
knob of butter	nuez de mantequilla
knucklebone (of pork)	hueso de codillo
knucklebone (of veal)	hueso de caña

L l

ladles	cucharones
lamb	cordero
lard	grasa de cerdo
larder	despensa
layer	capa
leaf	hoja
leeks	puerros
lemon	limón
lentils	lentejas
lettuce	lechuga
lid	tapadera
light	encender
lima bean	frijol
lime	lima
liquidize	triturar
liver	higado
loaf	barra

M m

marrow	calabaza
main course	plato principal
marinade	marinar
mash	hacer puré
mayonnaise	mayonesa

mead	aguamiel
measuring cup	taza para medir
measuring jug	jarra graduada
measuring spoon	cuchara de medir
meat	carne
meatball	albóndiga
meathook	gancho de carnicero
medium-sized	de tamaño mediano
melt	derretir
melted	derretido
melting point	punto de fusión
milk	leche
mince	carne picada
minced beef	ternera picada
mince pork	cerdo picado
mint	menta
mix	mezclar
mixer (food mixer)	batidora
mixing bowl	bol
molasses	melazaf
monkfish	rape
mortar	mortero
mulberry	mora
mushrooms	champiñones
mussels	mejillones
mustard	mostaza

N n

nectarine	nectarina
noodles	tallarines
non-fattening	no engordante
nourishing	nutritivo
nutmeg	nuez moscada

O o

oil	aceite
omelette (eggs only)	tortilla francesa
omelette (with potatoes)	tortilla
onion	cebolla
olive	aceituna
olive oil	aceite de oliva
orange	naranja
oregano	orégano
oven	horno
ovenproof	de horno
oxtail	rabo de buey
oyster	ostra

P p

pan	cazo
pancake	crepe
paprika	pimentón
parsley	perejil
partridge	perdiz
pasta	pasta
pasty	empanada
pâté	paté
pea	guisante
peach	melocotón
peanut	cacahuete, maní
peanut butter	mantequilla de cacahuete
peel	pelar
peeled	pelado
pepper	pimienta
peppercorns	granos de pimienta
pinch	pizca
pizza	pizza
pineapple	piña
plum	ciruela
poached	escalfado
poppyseed	semilla de amapola
pork	cerdo
pork fat	tocino
potato peeler	cosa para pelar patatas
potato starch	fécula
potatoes	patatas (or papa)

58

pour	verter
prawns	gambas
preservative	conservante
preserve	conservar
pretzel	galleta
prune	ciruela
pudding	budín
puff pastry	hojaldre
pulses	alubias
pumpkin	calabaza

Q q

quail	codorniz
quartered	cortado en cuatro
quince	membrillo

R r

rabbit	conejo
radish	rábano
raisin	pasa (de uva)
rare (meat)	poco hecho
raw	crudo
recipe	receta

recipe book	recetario
red pepper	pimiento rojo
red mullet	salmonete
reduce	reducir
remove	quitar
rennet	cuajo
rennin	rennina
rest	descansar
return	volver
rhubarb	ruibarbo
ribs	costillas
rice	arroz
rind	cáscara
rinse	limpiar con agua
ripe	maduro
roast	asado (asar)
roast beef	rosbi
roe	hueva
roll	rollito
roll out	aplanar
rosemary	romero
rub	frotar

S s
saffron	azafrán

sage	salvia
salmon	salmón
salt	sal
sandwich	bocadillo
sandwich toaster	sandwichera
sardines	sardinas
sauce	salsa
saucepan	cazo
sausage	salchicha
sausage meat	carne de salchicha
sauté	saltear
scald	escaldar
scrambled egg	huevos revueltos
sea bream	besugo
seal	sellar
seafood	mariscos
seasoning	condimento
seeds	semillas
self-raising	harina con levadura
sieve	tamizar
shallot	cebolleta
shapes	formas
shellfish	mariscos
shells	cáscaras
sherry	jerez
shopping list	lista de la compra
shoulder	paletilla
shrimp - (large)	langostino

shrimp - (medium)	camarón
shrimp - (small)	quisquilla
side	lado
silver foil	papel de aluminio
sieve	tamiz
simmer	cocinar a fuego lento
sirloin steak	solomillo
skim	desnatar
skimmed milk	leche desnatada
skin	piel
skinned	pelado
sliced	en trozos
sliced bread	pan de molde
smear	untar
smoked	ahumado
snack	un tentempié
snail	caracol
soak	remojar
soft drink	refresco
sour	agrio
sour cream	nata agri
spare ribs	costillas
spicy	picante
spinach	espinacas
spoon	cucharada
sprig	ramita
sprinkle	salpicar
squeeze	exprimir

squid	calamar
stale bread	pan duro
stalk	tallo
steak	bistec
steamer	vapor
stew	estofado
stiff	espeso
stir-fry	freír
stock	caldo
strain	colar
strainer	colador
strawberry	fresa
strips	tiritas
stuff	rellenar
stuffing	relleno
Sugar	azucar
sultana	pasa sultana
sweet	dulce
sweet and sour	agridulce
sweet basil	albahaca
sweetbreads	mollejas, lechecillas
sweetcorn	maíz tierno
sweeten	endulzar
sweetener	endulzante
sweet potato	boniato
syrup	almíbar

T t

tablespoon	cuchara
tangerine	tangerina
tartar sauce	salsa tártara
taste	sabor
teaspoon	cucharita
tender	tierno
tenderloin steak	solomillo
tepid	tibio
thick	grueso, espeso
thoroughly	completamente
thyme	tomillo
tie	atar
tin	lata
tinned	en lata
toasted	tostado
tofu	tofu, queso de soja
tomatoe	tomate
transfer	transferir
trickle	chorrear un poco
trim	cortar
trout	truc
turkey	pavo
turn	dar la vuelta
turn off	apagar

U u
unleavened (bread) pan sin levadura

V v
vanilla essence esencia de vainilla
vinegar vinagre
veal ternera
vodka vodka

W w
walnuts nueces
warm calentar
wash lavar
watercress berro
wedge pedazo grande
whipped cream nata montada
whisk batir
wild boar jabalí
wipe limpiar con un paño

Y y

yolks   yemas

Z z

zest   cáscara, peladura
zucchini   calabacín

Also by **Serge Seveau**:

Cryptic Poetry:

"Knowledge of less importance"

www.ingramcontent.com/pod-product-compliance
Lightning Source LLC
Chambersburg PA
CBHW071844020426
42331CB00007B/1850